The Little Angel Books Series

Crystals R for Kids

Written & Illustrated

by Leia A. Stinnett

Cover art by Leia Stinnett

ISBN 0-929385-92-6

Published by

StarChild Press
a division of

Light Technology
Publishing
P.O. Box 1526
Sedona, Arizona 86339
(520) 282-6523

Printed by

**MISSION
POSSIBLE
Commercial
Printing**

P.O. Box 1495
Sedona, AZ 86339

Hi, boys and girls!
My name is Chris Crystal. I am here to share some wonderful information about myself and other members of my family — Amy Amethyst, Rosey Rose Quartz, Charley Citrine and Sam Smokey Quartz.

Each of us has a special story to tell you about how we can help you feel better about yourself, how you can use us to help heal yourself and others, get better grades in school, feel closer to God and feel more loving toward yourself and other people in the world.

1

In this little workbook we will share some special ways you can work and play with us. We want you to have fun with us, but we also want you to understand that we really care about you and your happiness and growth.

Crystals and Stones — Where Did They Come From?

When our Earth was formed over millions of years ago, gases from deep within the earth's structure mixed with seawater that was 200 degrees in temperature and full of minerals. As the gases and seawater combined, the first crystals were formed.

It is believed that the ancient Lemurian and Atlantean peoples built huge pyramid structures with large crystals placed on top. Through these crystals, they were able to bring the energies from out in the universe to Earth.

These people used this power to operate their cities — for lighting, in the operation of machinery and equipment, in healing work and to communicate with their forefathers from another galaxy far away.

The Atlantean people realized how great the crystal power was. They began developing ways to use this power in making weapons to destroy other people.

But what happened was far from what they expected. This great power backfired, created a great explosion and Atlantis sank beneath the sea.

Before Atlantis was destroyed, a few of the very spiritual people of Atlantis programmed their great knowledge into certain crystals. In other words, they simply placed their thoughts into the crystals and the information has remained there

throughout the ages.

They sent these beautiful crystals deep within the earth where this information would stay buried until it was time for it to be discovered and used properly.

These wise people knew that some day it would be possible for other spiritual people to find these crystals and learn from them all about the great continent of Atlantis.

These crystals are called *record keepers*. On one of the faces of this type of crystal there is a small pyramid etched into the crystal itself. Do you have one in your collection?

A few people survived Atlantis' destruction. They traveled to Egypt, South America and Tibet where they built pyramids just like the ones they built in Atlantis. You can still see the remains of these pyramids if you visit any of these countries today.

Throughout history, many people of ancient cultures have used colored stones and crystals to cure specific illnesses, for power and for protection.

Mayan and American Indian people used crystals to diagnose and treat diseases and to see into their past and future lives.

Certain Indians from Mexico believed that if you led a good life, after you died your soul went inside a crystal. Then, any person who found this particular crystal would have good luck and good health during his/her lifetime. They also believed that the crystal would serve as their guide throughout life.

Today crystals are

used in wristwatches, computers, radio and television transmitters, lasers and other technical devices.

The crystal is popular because it has both negative and positive charges. It can vibrate to any electrical current in a very accurate way.

Crystals can also help us with our spiritual growth.

We use them in meditation, in protection and guidance. We can put them under our pillows at night so we can better understand our dreams.

We can also use crystals and stones to balance our body's energy system. Crystals can help us change our feelings from sad to glad, give us more energy, help us focus and concentrate and help us feel closer to God.

Crystals are light. They help bring more light into our lives.

The Parts of a Crystal

A quartz crystal has six sides on what is called the *body* of the crystal. These sides meet at the top in a sharp point called the *termination.*

In a single-terminated crystal there is only one point, or termination. The base is flat or ragged looking. This type of crystal grows out of rock. Only one point forms as it grows. In this type of crystal, energy comes into the crystal at its base and moves up and out of the termination.

In a double-terminated crystal there are two points, or terminations. These crystals grow in soft, sandy soil so the points can grow at both ends. In this type of crystal the energy flows in and out of the crystal at both ends.

This type of crystal is used to balance our *chakra energy* centers.

What Can Crystals Do?

• Crystals can amplify (make stronger) our thoughts and feelings.

For instance, you can sit right now and think about a happy thought. Be as happy as you can. Remember this feeling.

Now, hold a crystal in your hand and again, think about a happy thought. Be as happy as you can.

Do you feel even more happy now with the crystal helping you?

• Crystals can transform the molecular structure of anything they are placed in contact with.

Thus, when we hold or wear a crystal, it helps to balance our energy and heal our body by removing negative thoughts from our energy field.

- Crystals can store energy for us to use at a later time.

When you charge crystals in the sunlight, for example, you are putting more energy into the stones.

This energy will stay in the crystal until you are ready to use that energy in your meditation, healing or protection work.

- We can use crystals to transfer energy to another person. We call this *mental telepathy*, or sending our thoughts to another person.

Tumbled Gemstones

Agates: Translucent browns or grey microcrystalline quartz sometimes banded or mottled. The bright agates have been coloured: blue, green, teal, pink and red/brown. Believed to improve self esteem by making one more present. ♣

Amazonite: Opaque blue-green. Strengthens heart and physical body. Aids alignment of mental and etheric body. Good for expression and creativity. ♣

Amethyst: Light to dark violet quartz crystal. Purifies and dispels negativity. Used extensively in meditation. ♣

Aventurine: Green variety is quartz with sparkling chrome mica inclusions. It is said to promote health, tranquillity and positive attitudes. ♣

Bloodstone: Dark green with red. Once used to calm, ground, revitalize and reduce emotional stress. Stimulates movement of kundalini.

Blue Lace: Blue lace agate equates to a peaceful countenance and is used to support expression.

Fancy Jasper: Green, red and brown mixture. It helps align energies and is used for positive thinking.

Fancy Jasper: Clear, purple/green, soft. Improves absorption of essential nutrients. Grounds excess energy. Helps one to grasp higher ideals and advances the mind.

Fossil Jasper: Grey with tiny fossil inclusions. Brings one closer to nature with an appreciation of our evolution.

Fluorite: Clear, green and purple banded. The stone is known for its purifying and cleansing qualities. ♣

Hawk's Eye: Blue gray to blue green. Helps one gain perspectives in all physical realities.

Hematite: Shiny black iron ore. As a grounding stone it is used for original thinking and deflecting negativity. ♣

Iron Tigereye: Black and reddish striations. Grounds the physical being and assists in the acceptance of the body.

Howlite: White or dyed blues. Used for reflecting purity and assists in communication.

see over

Lapis:	Dark blue with streaks of pyrite. The stone of wisdom and used for telepathic communications.
Leopard Skin:	Form of Jasper with coloured swirls. It can be used for protection, regulation and balancing the body.
Lepidolite:	Pink to purple silicate. Contains lithium once used to calm the mind. Balances heart with mind.
Moonstone:	Cream to light brown. Enhances intuition. Relieves anxiety and helps reduce tendency to overreact emotionally.
Moss Agate:	Dark green with clear agate. Binds the energies of nature & assists in the balancing of the heart.
Obsidian:	Black, mahogany spotted or snowflake (spotted). Grounding stone with aspects of spirit (white) and body (reddish mahogany).
Picture Jasper:	Brown banded and mottled containing iron oxides.. Used for connection to the earth.
Quartz :	Clear/smoky crystalline or white/green. Considered solidified light. Amplifies, stores, transmits, conducts energy. Used in meditation. ♣
Quartz, dyed :	Opaque quartz which has been colored: amethyst, ruby, topaz yellow, tourmaline (green), coral, peridot (lime green), turquoise and sapphire (dark blue).
Red Jasper:	Red with light lines or mottled (brecciated). Supports the energy of procreation. ♣
Rhodonite:	Dark pink and black mottled. Important heart stone which will usher in the love force. ♣
Rose Quartz:	Pink quartz. True love stone. Promotes affinity for self and others through its affinity for the heart. ♣
Sodalite:	Dark blue with white lines. Sodium silicate. Assists in calming of the mind enabling one to see. ♣
Tigereye:	Brown silicate with lustrous golden yellow fibres. A power stone to help manifest one's desires.
Unakite:	Green & pink spotted granite. The colors are associated with healing of the heart.

♣ - Canadian Rocks

Telepathy Exercise

Choose a partner. Sit on the floor facing each other about one to two feet apart. Choose one person to be the sender, the other the receiver.

*The sender should hold a crystal with the flat base against his/her **third eye**. Point the tip of the crystal toward the receiver.*

The receiver should hold the point of the crystal to his/her third eye and the flat base pointing toward the sender.

Choose a color. The sender should send the color he/she chooses through the crystal to the receiver. Imagine the color passing from the sender's mind through the crystal like a beam of light to the receiver.

Then the receiver should play the role of sender and the sender, the receiver. Be sure to change the position of your crystals depending on whether you are the sender or receiver.

Remember: Not everyone can send or receive equally. Some of us are better senders. Some of us are better receivers.

Be happy with the great job you do in either case.

Selecting a Crystal

The best way to select a crystal or stone for yourself is to go to a crystal store and pick up the first one that seems to call to you.

Often, when you walk into a crystal store, you will feel like you want to walk to a certain corner of the room. You might feel that one particular crystal seems to be *winking* or *flashing* at you.

Hold the crystal in your left hand. Feel the *energy.*

Does the energy make you feel good? Does it make you tingle all over?

This is the crystal you should take home with you. It has some things to share with you.

If you don't feel the energy in your

left hand, try using your right hand.
In many cases, left-handed people can feel
the energy better in their right hand.
Right-handed people can feel the energy
better in their left hand.

When you pick up a crystal,
remember that it is possible many
people have held that same crystal.
Their energies will be held inside that
crystal until you clear them out.

To clear out other people's energy,
blow three times into the crystal before
you check out its energy. Then there will
be only your energy in the crystal.

In that way you will have an even
better feeling about whether or not you
want to buy this crystal for your collection.

Tuning in to Crystals and Stones

Hold your crystal or stone in your left hand (right hand if you are left-handed). Feel the energy in your body.

- Where does the energy go?
- Where does the energy stop?
- Does your body feel hot or cold?
- Do you feel lots of energy?
- Do you feel calm, peaceful, happy, sad?

Now place the crystal or stone on your third eye.

- What do you see?
- What do you hear?
- What do you feel?

Now place the crystal or stone on any part of your body where it feels comfortable.

- Why did you place it there?
- How did it make you feel when you placed it there?

You can do this exercise with each

stone or crystal that you buy so you have a better feeling for how you are to use the stones for yourself and in helping other people.

Cleansing and Charging Your Crystals and Stones

When you first buy a crystal or stone, remember that it has the energy of everyone who has ever touched it contained inside of it. In order for you to better work with the crystal — so you don't pick up other people's thoughts and feelings from the crystal — you should cleanse the other energies from the crystal or stone. Then it will be ready for you to work with it and place within it your own energies and thoughts.

There are many ways to cleanse and charge your crystals and stones.

• Place the crystals and stones in sea salt for two to seven days.

23

• Rinse the crystals and stones in cold running water. Place them in the sunlight or in the light of the full Moon for three hours. The sunlight will put a very strong energy into the stones. Moonlight will be softer, more gentle.

• Hold the crystal or stone to your third eye. Imagine energy going into the stone to make it clear. Imagine that the crystal or stone is empty, that there is no energy in it from anyone or anything else.

• Hold the crystal or stone in front of you. Blow real hard with your breath into the stone, imagining that all the energy you do not want inside of it is leaving.

When you charge the crystal or stone with sunlight or moonlight, you give it new power to focus, increase and direct energy when you work with it. It feels refreshed, like you feel when you wake up from a nice long nap.

Programming Your Crystals and Stones

To program your crystal means that you place inside the crystal or stone the thought that you want it to help you work on.

For example, if you want to heal yourself from a headache using the crystal or stone, you would think into the crystal or stone, *You are now programmed with healing energy for . . . (your name)*.

This makes the crystal or stone a stronger tool for you to use in healing yourself.

You can program your crystal for many purposes: meditation, to help you stay happy, to help you release negative or fearful thoughts and feelings, to help bring you good luck, better grades in school, healing energy for yourself and others, protection and so on.

26

To program your crystal or stone, hold it to your third eye and imagine with your mind what you want to put into the crystal or stone.

You can also hold the crystal or stone to your heart center and send loving thoughts into it about what you want to work on with the help of the crystal or stone.

You can blow three times with your breath into the crystal or stone. When you blow, imagine what you want to place inside the crystal. Keep thinking the thought until you feel the message is locked tightly inside the crystal or stone.

The programmed thought will stay in your crystal or stone until you cleanse it by using one of the ways mentioned before. Then it is ready for another thought of your choice to be programmed into it.

Introduction to the Crystal Family

I am Amy Amethyst. I am purple or violet in color, tapering to white or near white at my base in some instances.

I grow in clusters or in a group of stones just like me. We don't all look the same. Some of us are larger than others. We might be different shades of purple, but the cluster is my family. We grow together, work and play together and love each other, just as you do in your own family.

I can be found in different parts of the world, particularly in Mexico and Brazil.

I make a great companion at bedtime when you have trouble falling asleep. I am very calming and soothing. Put me under your pillow, and I will show you just how easy it is to fall asleep.

I am a great playmate during the day because I help you stay very loving —

not angry or hard to get along with.

I help you stay healthy. My energy, or vibration, helps you have a strong immune system so your body can fight off any disease that tries to come in.

I help you feel great all the time — day and night. I never tire of helping you. I know you will take good care of me.

Wash me in cold water or salt water once a week, or carefully pass me through the smoke from incense or sage. This will help me keep my own energy balanced.

Oh, by the way, please don't put me in the sunlight. You see, sunlight makes me fade from purple to white.

I am Rosey Rose Quartz. I am a very popular stone. When you hold me, you can feel the love I represent.

I am very helpful when you feel sad, lonely or angry. I help you feel loved because I *am* love. My beautiful pink color is the color of love.

I am a friendly stone, and I need a lot of loving care because that is what I am here to teach you — to love yourself, respect yourself and take good care of yourself.

Wear me over your heart, or carry me in your pocket. I will work very hard to see you have a happy day.

Sometimes, we feel we can't do something good enough, other people are better than we are. I can help you see just how special you really are.

I am Charley Citrine. I work wonders for stomachaches. Just place me on your tummy when it hurts, and I will make it feel better soon.

I am yellow to yellowish-brown in color. I like to think of myself as a golden ray of sunlight, beaming through the dark clouds of any fear you might have. I can show you there is

really nothing to be afraid of.

Think of something you are afraid of. Hold me in your left hand or lie down and place me on your tummy. Now, with your imagination see me as the golden Sun, shining brighter and brighter. Before you know it, your fear is trapped in my brilliant light. My light dissolves the fear. Your fear is gone forever.

Anytime you are afraid, just remember how much God loves you, how much He/She protects you, and think of the golden Sun.

I am Sam Smoky Quartz. I am grayish- to brownish-black in color.

My job is to make you feel calm, more connected to the Earth, more grounded.

I help you realize when you need something, all you have to do is ask God. God sees that you have all you need because He/She loves you.

I help you to be happy just the way you are — boy or girl, short or tall, thin or fat.

I help protect you from energies that are not positive, so you can feel good about yourself.

I am Chris Clear Quartz Crystal. I come in all shapes and sizes. I might have a point at one or both ends, or grow in a large cluster or family like cousin Amy Amethyst and my other family members. I can be found in many places of the world — Arkansas, Brazil, Mexico, California and Arizona, to name but a few.

My job includes: helping you balance your body's energy centers; changing negative thoughts to positive thoughts; and helping you bring more light into your body, so you stay healthier, happier and more loving.

I can tell you stories about earlier civilizations, because I store information inside of me, like you do in your brain.

I don't have a brain like you, but I am still able to store information in my structure just the same.

I am used in computers to help store information and in television and radio sets to help transmit messages and pictures. Energy passes through me. I can bring information in or send information out.

You can use me to send messages to your friends. Remember what you learned on pages 15 and 17.

Of course, you really don't have to use me to send messages with your mind. However, when you use me, the message you send will be stronger and your friend can more easily pick up your message.

Crystals as Jewelry

You can wear crystals and stones around your neck for protection against unhappy thoughts and feelings. While you wear or carry a crystal or stone, it helps keep all your body's energies aligned and balanced, so you feel great and have lots more energy.

You can wear any colored stone you wish. One day you might choose to wear a red stone. Another day you might choose a green stone, depending on how you are feeling.

Let your *intuition* tell you what color stone to wear. See how much better you feel as the day goes by.

Crystals are worn as pendants

around your neck, as rings, bracelets and earrings. No matter where you place the crystals on your body, they will affect your energy in a positive way.

Crystals in Healing

If you have a pain in a certain part of your body, you can place a crystal or stone on the area to take away the pain on your body, or to help someone else or a pet.

If you use a crystal, you can place the base of the crystal on the part of the body that hurts. Point the tip of the crystal out, so you are sending the excess energy of that part of the body appearing as pain out through the tip of the crystal, out of your body.

Try this exercise the next time you have a headache. Watch your headache disappear in just a few minutes.

You can use your intuition to choose colored stones to place on your body

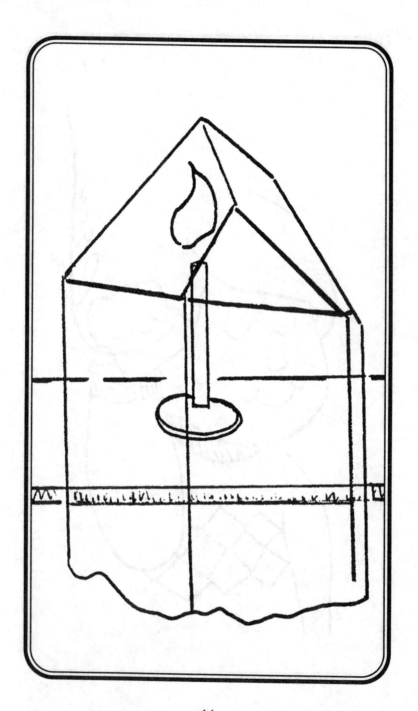

when there is a pain or a problem, or when you are not feeling well.

There are stones for sore throats, fevers, stomachaches, headaches and other ailments.

Place all of your colored stones and crystals on the table. Allow your mind to choose the one(s) you need.

Crystals in Meditation

When you meditate, try holding a crystal in your hand. The crystal will help you relax and quiet your mind.

Try lighting a candle. Hold the crystal up in front of the candle flame. Keep your eyes open and stare inside the crystal at the lights and colors until your eyes want to close naturally. See how long you can hold the colors in the center of your forehead behind your eyes — in your third-eye vision.

As you close your eyes, imagine

you can float right through an open doorway and into your crystal.

You are now inside your crystal. It is like a little crystal house.

Look all around the inside of your crystal. Look at all the colors inside.

• What do you see? Now feel your crystal. Feel the floor and the walls. How does the crystal feel?

• Listen very carefully. What do you hear inside your crystal? Do you hear any sounds at all? Do you hear music?

• What does it smell like inside your crystal?

• What does it taste like inside your crystal? You might even want to imagine you are placing your tongue on the walls of the crystal to find out.

Now, sit quietly inside your crystal and just be one with it.

Feel the peace all around you.

Feel the energy of the crystal as it makes you feel more energized and happier, more at peace, more one with God.

When you are ready, let your body float back out of the doorway of the crystal, back into your room, into the physical body. Then open your eyes very slowly.

- What did you think about your journey?
- What did you see?
- What did you feel?
- What did you hear?
- What did you smell?
- What did you taste?

Draw a picture of your experience during the crystal meditation.

Balancing Your Chakras with Crystals and Stones

The chakras are seven very special energy centers, which help keep us happy and healthy. Each chakra center is responsible for some type of sensing with the physical body. Each chakra is responsible for a different type of emotion or feeling.

The *first (root) chakra* is concerned with our needs to survive on Earth — having a house to live in, enough good, nourishing food, clothing and loving parents to take care of us. It helps us feel grounded to the Earth.

The *second chakra* is concerned with our ability to feel energy on the outside of our body, feeling good about being a boy or a girl and being able to use our creative energy.

The *third chakra* helps us see that we have a high level of energy at all

51

times. It helps us keep our personal power, to take care of ourselves and not let other people boss us around, or make us do things we do not want to do.

The *fourth chakra* is concerned with our emotions and touch. It helps us heal those things that happened during childhood at some time, which might have been hurtful to us in some way.

The *fifth chakra* helps us hear energy or voices or our spirit guides and guardian angels. It helps us talk with our parents, teachers and friends.

The *sixth chakra* helps us see energy with our mind's eye.

The *seventh (crown) chakra* helps us stay connected with God.

One great way to keep your chakras balanced and happy is by using crystals and stones that are the same color as the chakra you are placing the stones on.

For example, on your third eye, which is indigo, or purple, you would place a dark blue or purple stone.

On your *solar plexus*, which is yellow, you would place a yellow stone.

The Most Common Stones to Use Are:

First (root) chakra: red jasper or black onyx.

Second chakra: orange carnelian.

Third chakra: yellow citrine.

Fourth chakra: rose quartz or green aventurine.

Fifth chakra: turquoise or blue-lace agate.

Sixth chakra: amethyst or sodalite.

Seventh (crown) chakra: clear quartz crystal, amethyst or yellow citrine.

Chakra Balancing Exercise

You can place the stones on your body by yourself or have a parent or friend help you.

It is important to lie down in a quiet place to do the crystal balances, so you can relax and feel the energy of the stones as they work on the chakra centers of your body.

To begin, place the clear quartz with the point, or termination, touching the top of your head. Place the blue or purple stone on your third eye.

Then place stones on your throat, heart, solar plexus, second chakra and root chakra.

Leave the stones on your body for about 15 minutes. Should one or more of the stones fall off your body, leave them off. The stones know better than we do when they have completed their job.

You can place the stones on your body

whenever you feel a bit out of touch with the world — nervous, hyperactive, angry, sad — like you feel bad all over; when you feel stuck places, or globs, in your body; when you can't concentrate on your school work and so on.

Your intuition will let you know when it is time for a chakra balance.

Remember: Listen carefully to your body.

When you have completed the chakra balance, you might want to place your stones in cold running water and sunlight to cleanse, recharge and refresh their energies.

Take good care of your stones. They will always take very good care of you.

They are just like loving little friends . . . very special friends.

What did you feel in your chakra centers while the stones were on your body?

First Chakra: _____

_____

Second Chakra: _____

_____

Third Chakra: _____

_____

Fourth Chakra: _____

_____

Fifth Chakra: _____

_____

Sixth Chakra: _____

_____

Seventh Chakra: _____

_____

• In which chakra did you feel the most energy? _____
• In which chakra did you feel the least energy? _____
• What is your favorite crystal? _____

- Why? _____
- What is your favorite colored stone?

  _____

- Why? _____

Crystals and Stones to the Rescue

Headache: Place clear quartz crystal, citrine, amethyst on crown.

Sore throat, cough, fever: place turquoise, blue-lace agate, aquamarine on throat.

Eye problem or earache: place sodalite or amethyst on third eye.

Stomachache, flu, feeling tired, allergies, muscle cramps: place yellow citrine, tiger's eye, bloodstone, rutilated quartz on third chakra.

Sadness, anger, hurtful feelings: place rose quartz, green aventurine, bloodstone on heart chakra.

What are your favorite stones to use when you are not feeling well?

Like a diamond in the sky,
My love & light shines down tonight,
And holds you in my tender care.
No harm shall come, it wouldn't dare!

I am a friend, no matter what.
I don't punish or hurt or shout.
I help you grow to God's own love,
And point the way to Heaven above.

Little one, sleep on tonight,
For I am here to light up the night.
Though small might I be, I have much to share.
As you reach for the stars,
please know I am there.

— Your friend, Chris

About the Author

The '80s were a decade of self-discovery for Leia Stinnett after she began researching many different avenues of spirituality. In her profession as a graphic designer she had become restless, knowing there was something important she had to do outside the materiality of corporate America.

In August 1986 Leia had her first contact with Archangel Michael when he appeared in a physical form of glowing blue light. A voice said, "I am Michael. Together we will save the children."

In 1988 she was inspired by Michael to teach spiritual classes in Sacramento, California, the Circle of Angels. Through these classes she had the opportunity to work with learning-disabled children, children of abuse and those from dysfunctional homes.

Later Michael told her, "Together we are going to write the Little Angel Books." To date Leia and Michael have created thirteen Little Angel Books that present various topics of spiritual truths and principles. The books proved popular among adults as well as children.

The Circle of Angels classes have been introduced to several countries around the world and across the U.S., and Leia and her husband Douglas now have a teacher's manual and training program for people who wish to offer spiritual classes to children. Leia and Michael have been interviewed on Canadian Satellite TV and have appeared on NBC-TV's *Angels II – Beyond the Light*, which featured their Circle of Angels class and discussed their books and Michael's visit.

The angels have given Leia and Douglas a vision of a new educational system without competition or grades — one that supports love and positive self-esteem, honoring all children as the independent lights they are. Thus they are now writing a curriculum for the new "schools of light" and developing additional books and programs for children.